JAPAN

by Max Winter

The Child's World

Published by The Child's World®
1980 Lookout Drive • Mankato, MN 56003-1705
800-599-READ • www.childsworld.com

Acknowledgments
The Child's World®: Mary Berendes, Publishing Director
Red Line Editorial: Editorial direction
The Design Lab: Design
Amnet: Production

Design element: Shutterstock Images
Photographs ©: Shutterstock Images, cover (left top),
cover (left center), cover (left bottom), cover (right), 5, 6–7,
11, 13, 21, 25; Sean Pavone/Shutterstock Images, 8, 15;
iStockphoto, 12, 14, 20, 22, 24, 26, 27, 30; Ed Stock/
iStockphoto, 17; Aleksandar Todorovic/Shutterstock Images,
23; Colin Ewington/iStockphoto, 28

ISBN 9781634070515
LCCN 2014959730

Printed in the United States of America
Mankato, MN
July, 2015
PA02268

ABOUT THE AUTHOR
Max Winter has written
and edited many books
about social studies
and science for young
readers. The subjects of
these books have ranged
from the Statue of
Liberty to building one's
own radio.

TABLE OF CONTENTS

ARCTIC
OCEAN

ATLANTIC
OCEAN

PACIFIC
OCEAN

INDIAN
OCEAN

PACIFIC
OCEAN

JAPAN

SCALE

0   1000 Miles

0   1000 KM

N
W   E
S

SOUTHERN
OCEAN

JAPAN

1965

日本郵便

10

Japan has many mountains. They cover about 80 percent of the country's land. About 60 of the mountains are active volcanoes.

CHAPTER 1

WELCOME TO JAPAN!

↖ Candles inside snow houses light up the winter night.

It is a dark, cold night. Snow covers the ground. All around, lights are glowing in the dark. The lights come from small snow houses called *kamakuras*. People have built them for the Yokote Kamakura Festival.

This festival has been celebrated for 400 years. It takes place each February in Yokote, Japan. It marks the end of New Year festivities. Children invite people passing by into their *kamakuras*. There, they eat rice cakes and visit.

Each *kamakura* also has an **altar**. It honors the water gods. People leave rice cakes at the altars. They hope this offering will please the gods, who will then provide plenty of water in the coming year.

The *kamakuras* are only one of many ancient traditions in Japan. It is a nation with a long history. Japan has been a country for 2,000 years. It is the world's oldest **monarchy**.

At one time, Japan was one of the world's most powerful countries. Japan's emperors wanted to rule many lands. They trained a strong army. The army conquered other lands for Japan.

By the 1900s, Japan controlled many parts of Asia. Japan was not able to keep this control, though. The countries Japan ruled slowly gained their freedom.

Today, Japan is a modern nation. It is a center of technology, education, and culture. Its people still follow ancient traditions, but they also have adopted modern customs.

The Japanese balance traditions with modern life. It is common to see people wearing traditional *kimonos* in the middle of a modern city.

CHAPTER 2

THE LAND

Mount Fuji is a volcano. It last erupted in 1707.

Japan is a group of many islands. They are in the Pacific Ocean, just east of Asia. The four main islands are Honshu, Hokkaido, Kyushu, and Shikoku.

Honshu is Japan's largest island. About 80 percent of Japan's people live there. Mountains rise across much of the island. The largest is Mount Fuji. It is 12,388 feet (3,776 m) tall.

Hokkaido is Japan's most northern island. Few people live there. The island is wild and beautiful. It has mountains with snowy peaks. Wildflowers bloom on the mountain slopes in the spring. Forests are home to red foxes, deer, and cranes.

Kyushu is in southern Japan. There are many smaller islands near it. Kyushu has many hot springs. They are places where warm water from underground bubbles to the surface. Many people enjoy sitting in the warm water. They believe it has healing powers.

Shikoku is the smallest of Japan's four main islands. There are many mountains and thick forests there. It also has good land for farming. Farmers grow crops such as rice, wheat, and oranges. Their farms are usually on the coast or along river valleys.

The weather in Japan is often mild. The areas closer to the ocean are warmer. The inland areas are cooler. High in the mountains, it can snow heavily during the winter.

In the fall, Japan has strong storms. They are called typhoons. Typhoons bring wind and heavy rain to areas along the coast. Typhoons can be dangerous. The rains cause flooding, and the winds can destroy entire towns.

Japan also has more than 1,000 earthquakes every year. In 2011, an underwater earthquake in the Pacific Ocean created a **tsunami.** It destroyed cities and homes. The damage was widespread. Countries across the globe gave money, workers, and supplies to help Japan rebuild.

Steam rises off a hot spring in Beppu, Japan. Beppu is on Kyushu and it has 3,750 hot springs.

Japan's land can be a good resource. It is excellent for growing rice. The Japanese people make use of the water surrounding their islands, too. They catch large amounts of fish. The rice and fish are important to Japan's **economy**. Japan sells these goods to other countries.

Japan is famous for its cherry blossoms. Each spring, many cherry trees bloom with pink flowers. They blanket the country in soft, pink petals.

Much of Japan's farmland is used to produce rice. The wet fields that rice grows in are called paddies.

CHAPTER 3

GOVERNMENT AND CITIES

The Sumida River flows through Tokyo and empties into Tokyo Bay.

More than 90 percent of Japanese people live in large cities. Many live in Honshu. Tokyo is on Honshu's east coast. It is Japan's capital and largest city. More than 35 million people live in and around Tokyo.

Tokyo is located on the Sumida River. The Imperial Palace is in the center of the city. It is where Japan's emperor lives. The palace is surrounded by government buildings and the city's business district.

Tokyo is Japan's most important city. It has banks, television stations, newspapers, and universities. Electronics such as smartphones, computers, and televisions are made

Tokyo is a crowded city. Each 1 square mile (2.6 sq km) is home to about 11,000 people.

in Tokyo. These electronics are sold in Japan and in other countries.

Osaka is another important Japanese city. It has many factories. They make goods such as appliances, electronics, and textiles. Other factories make paper or print books. Osaka is also known for its universities, and it is a center of the arts.

Japan is ruled by a central government. The leader of the government is the prime minister. The prime minister works with the Diet. The Diet is group of people who make laws for the country.

Japan has an emperor, too. The emperor has not led the country for many years. Instead, the emperor is a symbol of Japan. He reminds people of Japan's past and participates in important ceremonies.

The Diet meets in Tokyo. All Japanese adults over age 21 can vote for the lawmakers who represent them in the Diet.

Japan has a strong economy. It produces many products sold in other countries. These products include electronics, cars, and food such as rice and fruit. These **exports** bring money into Japan.

Japan's currency

Japan's flag

FUN FACT

ONE WORLD · MANY COUNTRIES

According to tradition, Japan's first emperor took the throne in 660 BC. His name was Jimmu.

GLOBAL CONNECTIONS

Today, Japan actively trades goods. It sells products to many countries around the world and purchases them, too. But for a long time, it did not do so.

Japan once ruled many countries, both large and small. The rulers of Japan invaded countries all over the world and took them over. Japan's army was mighty and fierce. But then countries began to fight back against Japan.

Japan's rulers did not like the involvement of other countries. So, they closed the country to foreigners. No one was allowed into the country from outside Japan. Goods were not bought from other countries, nor were they sold to other countries. The country remained this way until the mid-1800s, when leaders began to open up Japan slowly.

Today, Japan buys many of its goods from other countries. And the goods made in Japan can be found all over the world. Japan is once again an important part of the world community.

CHAPTER 4

PEOPLE AND CULTURES

Families are important to people in Japan.

Approximately 127 million people live in Japan. Nearly all the people in Japan are Japanese. Few immigrants live there. Hokkaido has a small group of **indigenous** people. They are called they Ainu.

A gate called a *torii* marks the entrance to a Shinto shrine. A *torii* always has two rails on top and is often painted red.

Japan's two major religions are Buddhism and Shinto. Shinto is Japan's oldest religion. In Shinto, many gods called *kami* rule nature. People worship *kami* at **shrines**. Buddhism is based on the teachings of Buddha. Shinto and Buddhist beliefs often overlap and mix in Japan.

Japanese culture has many unique customs. For example, when people meet they bow to each other. It is a sign of respect. The deeper people bow, they more respect they show.

Another custom is removing shoes before entering homes. Inside, people wear slippers called *uwabaki*. The slippers cover a person's feet without tracking in dirt as regular shoes would.

Students practice martial arts in schools called *dojos*.

Many hosts provide slippers near the front door for their guests.

Japanese culture also includes martial arts. They began with Japanese warriors called samurai. The samurai trained for war using exercises to strengthen their minds and bodies. These exercises became modern martial arts such as karate and judo.

Sumo wrestling also began in Japan. The wrestlers are strong and often very large. They stand in a ring covered with sand. To win, one wrestler must force the other out of the ring. Or, he must force his opponent to touch the ground with any body part.

Theater is another important part of Japanese culture. In *Noh* theater, actors wear masks. The stage is simple with few decorations. Two or three performers dance to slow music. Kabuki is much different. The stage is colorful and has special effects, such as trap doors. The actors wear fancy costumes, wigs, and face paint.

Japanese people celebrate many holidays. One of the most important is New Year's Day. It is celebrated on January 1. People believe that watching the sunrise that morning will bring good luck. Families decorate their doors with pine and bamboo. They also go to shrines and temples, as well as visit friends and family.

Most people in Japan speak Japanese. The language is written in letters called characters. Some characters represent sounds, while others represent words or ideas. Japanese characters are read from right to left.

FUN FACT

CHAPTER 5

DAILY LIFE

The inside of this traditional Japanese home has sliding doors, tatami mats, and paper windows.

Daily life in Japan begins at home. Traditional Japanese homes are called *minka*. Most *minka* are made of wood. Windows are made of heavy paper. It offers privacy but still lets in light.

Inside, sliding doors can open and close to change the size of a room. *Tatami* mats made from **rushes** cover the floors.

Japanese homes do not have much furniture. People often sit directly on the floor. At night, people set up **futon** mattresses for sleep. In the morning, they store the mattresses in closets.

Meals in Japan are served at low tables. People sit on cushions on the ground when they eat. They eat their food with chopsticks. If soup is served, people can sip it directly from the bowl.

Most Japanese meals include rice or noodles. Another common dish is miso soup. It is flavored with soybean paste

A family enjoys a meal while sitting on the floor.

People usually wear wooden sandals called *zori* or *geta* with their *kimonos*. The sandals are easy to slip off when entering a home.

Many Japanese meals include seafood. Sometimes people eat thinly sliced pieces of raw fish. It is often served with rice. This is type of food is called *sushi*.

Clothing in Japan is similar to that worn in the United States. For special occasions, a person may wear a *kimono*. It is a long, flowing robe. A wide sash called an *obi* keeps the *kimono* closed. *Kimonos* are worn by both men and women.

When men and boys wear *kimonos*, they wear a jacket over the top. It is called *haori*.

The Shinkansen Bullet Train in Japan can travel at speeds of up to 200 miles (320 km) per hour.

Japanese people often travel long distances to get to work. Many take trains. Japan has some of the fastest, most advanced trains in the world. Bridges and ferries connect the islands.

The islands that make up Japan have a long history. They are filled with ancient religions, traditions, and culture. Today, Japan's people stay true to their traditions while adopting new ideas.

DAILY LIFE FOR CHILDREN

In Japan, school is taken very seriously. Throughout their education, Japanese schoolchildren spend 240 days out of the year in school. That is two-thirds of the year!

Japanese school years are divided into three terms. This means that students have breaks, but they aren't summer breaks or winter breaks like students in the United States have.

Many of the high schools in Japan are private. They are small and often expensive. At the end of high school, all Japanese students have to take a test. This test is very important. It determines whether a student gets into a good university.

There are many choices of schools. Japan has more than 700 universities.

FUN FACT

Every day, children in Japan help clean their schools for 20 to 30 minutes. This job is called souji. It teaches students how to clean and how to work as a team.

ONE WORLD · MANY COUNTRIES

1965

FAST FACTS

Population: 127 million

Area: 145,925 square miles (377,915 sq km)

Capital: Tokyo

Largest Cities: Tokyo, Yokohama, and Osaka

Form of Government: Constitutional Monarchy

Language: Japanese

Trading Partners: China, the United States, and South Korea

Major Holidays: Japanese New Year and Constitution Day

National Dish: Sushi (raw fish, rice, seaweed, and other ingredients)

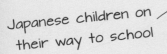

Japanese children on their way to school

GLOSSARY

altar (AWL-tur) An altar is a table or raised area that is used for a religious ceremony. The snow homes in Yokote each have an altar.

economy (ih-KON-uh-mee) An economy is how a country runs its industry, trade, and finance. Electronics are important to Japan's economy.

exports (ek-SPORTS) Exports are goods sold to another country. Cars are one of Japan's exports.

futon (FOO-tahn) A futon is a small mattress that is used on the floor or in bed frames. Sleeping on a futon is common in Japan.

indigenous (in-DIH-juh-nuhs) Indigenous means naturally coming from a particular region. The Ainu are indigenous to Hokkaido.

monarchy (MON-ur-kee) A monarchy is a government ruled by a monarch, such as a king, queen, or emperor. Japan is the world's oldest monarchy.

rushes (RUSH-ez) Rushes are tall plants that grow in marshes. *Tatami* mats are made of woven rushes.

shrines (shrynz) Shrines are places where people worship gods. Japan has many Shinto shrines.

tsunami (tsoo-NAH-mee) A tsunami is a large and destructive ocean wave created by earthquakes or underwater volcanoes. A tsunami in Japan caused terrible damage in 2011.

To Learn More

BOOKS

Florence, Debbi Michiko. *Japan: Over 40 Activities to Experience Japan.* Nashville, TN: Williamson Books, 2009.

Hale, Christy. *The East-West House: Noguchi's Childhood in Japan.* New York: Lee & Low Books, 2009.

Sakade, Florence. *Japanese Children's Favorite Stories.* Tokyo: Tuttle, 2013.

WEB SITES

Visit our Web site for links about Japan: **childsworld.com/links**

Note to Parents, Teachers, and Librarians: We routinely verify our Web links to make sure they are safe and active sites. So encourage your readers to check them out!

Index